MIKE MURRAY

Published by Influence Resources
1445 N. Boonville Ave.
Springfield, Missouri 65802

Cover and interior design by Prodigy Pixel, www.prodigypixel.com

ISBN: 978-1-62912-157-4
17 16 15 14 • 1 2 3 4 5

Printed in the United States of America

CONTENTS

Week 3: Listen

Week 4: Follow

THE NEXT CHAPTER: STAN STEWARD
FEBRUARY 12, 1962–AUGUST 2, 2013

"I tell you the truth, unless a kernel of wheat
is planted in the soil and dies, it remains alone.
But its death will produce many new kernels—a
plentiful harvest of new lives." —John 12:24, NLT

Stan is home now.

On Friday evening, August 2, 2013, just before sundown in Istanbul, he finished his race—and he finished well. Through the pain, through the discomfort, until his final hours, he sang praises to his Lord and offered prayers on behalf of the people he loved . . . as in living, so in dying.

Cancer destroyed Stan's body, but it couldn't touch his joy, his peace, or his passion to know Jesus and to make Him known. Now, he sees his Lord face to face.

Stan's prayer in his final eleven months was identical to his prayer in the preceding five decades. It's a simple prayer: to God be the glory. In a life lived for Him, to God be the glory. In a death offered to Him, to God be the glory. Stan's hope, his conviction, was that his dying out loud would draw his Turkish family to the One who sustained and comforted him.

Job 14:5 (NLT) says, "You have decided the length of our lives. You know how many months we will live, and we are not given a minute longer." The timing of Stan's death was not lost on his Muslim friends. They were quick to point out its significance: Stan died peacefully at dusk on the final Friday of Ramazan, the month of fasting. This night is the holiest in Islam, an evening known as the Night of Power. Stan's friends and neighbors recognized this moment as a great honor, a sign of God's love for their brother who had loved and prayed for them, a sign that he found favor in God's eyes.

And so, on Sunday afternoon, as dozens of the Stewards' Turkish and American friends gathered to say good-bye, we hugged, we wept, we even laughed a little. We remembered Stan's love of family and friends, his wit, his embrace of every moment of life.

But, as Stan would have it, even though his funeral was *for* him, it was not *about* him. The focus, as Stan would have it, was on Jesus . . . as in living, so in dying.

Stan, Ann, Elle, and Stanley wanted this moment to be more than a remembrance of a full life well lived. They wanted their Turkish family to meet the source of Stan's hope, to come face to face with the Resurrection and Life. The songs we sang that day, the prayers we prayed, the message we heard all pointed to the hope we can have: eternal life freely given by the One who conquered the grave. No fear in death.

A day later, under a cloudless sky on a wind-whipped hillside high above the Euphrates River in central Turkey, a couple dozen friends surrounded Ann, Elle, and Stanley as Stan's body reached its final resting place. It's a simple grave in an old Armenian cemetery on the edge of a village he loved.

Again, the good news of Jesus was proclaimed in a corner of the world where it is seldom heard. Again, New Testaments in the Turkish language were given to Stan's dear Turkish friends. Before Stan's casket was lowered into the rocky soil, one final hymn rang out: "Great Is Thy Faithfulness."

Our God is faithful to fulfill His promises. A kernel of wheat is planted in the soil and dies, but its death will produce a plentiful harvest. We wait for that day.

—Mike Murray, Istanbul, August 2013

STAND IN THE GAP

I looked for someone among them who would
build up the wall and stand before me in the gap
on behalf of the land so I would not have to destroy it,
but I found no one. Ezekiel 22:30

"Oh God, I stand in the gap today on behalf of Turks.
God, raise up men and women who are so desperate
to reach them that they feel as if they are going to die
if they don't." —Stan's prayer journal

You've read *Dying Out Loud*, or you've watched the DVD, and maybe you're wondering: *Now what?* The Steward family's story of obedience and sacrifice has captured your attention, and now you want to pray for Muslims. Or you might be hungry to spend time in the presence of Jesus, to hear His voice. Perhaps you sense that God is calling you to proclaim the good news in Turkey or elsewhere in the Muslim world.

Perhaps you've come to a point of total surrender to God's will: *Lord, I will go anywhere and do anything for You, no matter the cost.*

This journal provides a framework to help you pray for Turks and other unreached people groups in Turkey. It creates an environment to help you abide in Jesus, surrender to His will, hear His voice, and follow where He leads.

Stan's core message in *Dying Out Loud* will be our guide: "You were created for a purpose. God has a plan that involves you, and if you don't complete the tasks He has for you, they may very well go undone. Seek Him with all your heart! Be open to the plan He has for you! While it may involve sacrifice, it will also fill the hole inside of you that cries out for meaning."[1]

The twenty-eight daily readings are loosely organized into four weekly themes: abide, surrender, listen, and follow. Abiding in Christ—the Vine—is foundational to all else, and each theme builds on the previous one. As you progress through the journal, please pray each day for the land that Stan and Ann committed their lives to.

On the pages that follow, you will find three resources to help you do this. The first, "How to Pray for Turkey," is a list of twelve kingdom prayers that are especially relevant in the Muslim world. Please incorporate some or all of these prayers as you stand in the gap over the next twenty-eight days. Next, Ann has provided a detailed description of Stan's prayer time as well as her own. Feel free to borrow or adapt any elements that might enrich your own prayer time.

Welcome to the Dying Out Loud challenge.

HOW TO PRAY FOR TURKEY

Turkey is home to about 75 million people, and 99.5 percent of them are members of Muslim people groups. This means they have virtually no access to the gospel. Among the 53 million ethnic Turks in the country, only a few thousand are followers of Jesus. As you pray for Turkey and Turks, please remember the other unreached people groups as well, including Kurmanji Kurds (8 million), Turkish-speaking Kurds (5.8 million), Zaza-Dimlis (1.1 million), Lebanese Arabs (1.1 million), and Kabardians (1.1 million). For more information about the unreached peoples of Turkey, visit JoshuaProject.net.

Pray for laborers: Jesus told us to pray that the Lord would raise up laborers (diligent workers) for the harvest fields. Please pray that God would raise up missionaries from all over the world to plant the church together in Turkey (Matthew 9:37–38).

Pray for the conviction of sin: It is only through the knowledge of one's sinful state and subsequent repentance, which lead one to turn to Jesus, that a person is saved. Pray that the people of Turkey would feel and know the burden of sin and would come to Jesus for forgiveness and salvation (Matthew 11:28–30).

Pray for the cross to be unveiled: False religions and deceptive ideologies have blinded men and women from every group of people to the truths of the gospel. Please pray that God would unveil the cross and that the veil on the minds and spirits of the people of Turkey would be taken away (2 Corinthians 3:16–17).

Pray for faith and against fear: The Bible says that God has given His followers a spirit of power. Pray that believers among the Turks would be set free from a spirit of fear of what may come and would boldly proclaim the truth of the gospel (2 Timothy 1:6–8).

Pray for the Word of God to rise: God's Word is so much more powerful than anything we can say; it is a mighty lion that needs to be unleashed. Please pray for the Word of God (in written, oral, musical, and dramatic forms) to be translated and to rise among the unreached people groups of Turkey (Isaiah 55:10–11).

Pray that God will pour out His Spirit on all flesh: God has promised to pour out His Spirit on all flesh—men and women, young and old, rich and poor. Please pray that God would pour out His Spirit on the people of Turkey—that they would see dreams and visions of Jesus and would be powerfully saved and empowered to be His witnesses (Joel 2:28–32).

Pray that Jesus would unite the body of Christ: It is Jesus' desire that His followers be in one accord. Please pray that God would unite the body of Christ. Pray that Christians from around the world would work together to reach Turkey and that the people groups of Turkey would be joined to the body of Christ (John 17:20–23).

Pray for good soil: Pray that the hearts of the people of Turkey would be like good soil, ready to hear the gospel and respond (Mark 4:1–20).

Pray for peace: The Bible tells us to pray for the peace of Jerusalem (Psalm 122:6) and for the people among whom we live (1 Timothy 2:1–4). Pray that the people of Turkey would experience peace not only in their nation but also in their hearts. Pray for the peace that results when men and women are reconciled with God (John 14:27). Pray for women and men of peace (Luke 10:6) among the Turks and other unreached peoples of Turkey.

Pray for bold proclamation: Pray that believers in Turkey would proclaim the message of the gospel clearly, making the most of every opportunity God places before them (Colossians 4:2–5).

Pray against works-based salvation and legalism: Plead that the Turks will understand that hope for forgiveness and acceptance with God is available only through Jesus' work on the cross (1 Corinthians 1:18).

Pray for joy in persecution: Church history tells us that the church grows the most when persecution is present. Pray that the believers in Turkey will endure persecution in a Christlike manner and will give their lives for the sake of the gospel if necessary (1 Peter 2:21–23).

—Adapted from "Kingdom Prayers" in *Live Dead Joy*[2]

STAN'S PRAYER TIME

BY ANN STEWARD

How did Stan pray? Passionately!

Every morning, he went into his office with a mug of coffee, closed the door, put on worship music, and prayed for an hour or two. He followed various Bible reading schedules over the years, always trying to keep it fresh. The last couple of years he read the New Testament and listened to the Old Testament.

One part of his morning devotions that makes me smile even as I write this is that Stan had a very personal relationship with the Lord. He was also an extrovert and had to encourage others by sharing what the Lord was doing. He often came out of his office to share with the kids or me something the Lord had said to him, or he would call or write someone when the Lord put them on his heart. With that same exuberance, he headed to the streets to share the love of the Lord with his friends.

Stan changed his positions throughout his prayer time. He started reading his devotionals in his chair, moved to Bible reading on the traditional floor cushions, but interceded on a prayer rug, either on his knees or on his face before the Lord. He had lists of names that he called out before the Lord every day. He started with the kids and me, then family and friends, and then the lost around him and around the world.

Late in the afternoon, Stan would again close his office door to study and pray for thirty minutes to an hour.

Family altar was always an important part of Stan's daily prayers. Our family devotions have taken a lot of different forms over the years. When the kids were babies, it was short: a child on each of our laps, a simple Bible story, and children's worship songs. As they reached toddler stage, it was more interactive. We had a basket of props and a few dress-up items for the kids to act out a Bible story. We also wanted our kids to learn the hymns. To keep their attention, we put actions to the songs. I can still picture the kids marching around the living room to the hymn "We're Marching to Zion" or pretending to pass around food to the hymn "Come and Dine." We tried to keep it age-specific and fun.

As the years went on, family altar continued to evolve, but it was always an important time of prayer. Our kids were part of the ministry. We didn't just inform them about "our" ministry but relied on them to be part of our team. Each evening we gathered on our bed and shared the ins and outs of the day, how God had answered prayers from the morning and how we needed to pray for the coming day. We continued to sing the hymns, thankful for Elle's beautiful alto and Stanley's bass voices to carry us along. Stan would lead us all in prayer for one another and for the Lord's work.

MY PRAYER TIME

BY ANN STEWARD

I want to abide with the Lord constantly. I start my day by reading a Psalm and spending a moment in prayer with the Lord before I get out of bed, but the bulk of my prayer time comes after a shower and breakfast. I want to be alert, ready, and anticipating a communion time with the Lord. I gather my Bible, devotionals, a pen, and writing pad, and I start my day with one to two hours of prayer. As I sit down without my writing pad, I wonder in anticipation: *What will I hear from the Lord today?*

Why do I write things down? Whether it's due to age or a difficult time remembering things, I've found that if I record things that have special meaning to me during my prayer time, I'm better able to remember them and meditate on them throughout the day.

I begin by quieting my heart, acknowledging who the Lord Almighty really is, and praising Him. I expect that He will communicate with me and teach me. My favorite Bible verse is Exodus 33:13: "Now therefore, if I have found favor in your sight, please show me now your ways, that I may know you, in order to find favor in your sight" (ESV).

Reading a devotional helps me at the beginning of my prayer time. I use many different devotionals, and some of my favorites are *Streams in the Desert* by Lettie Cowman, *My Daily Homily, Morning and Evening* by Charles H. Spurgeon, and *God's Best Secrets* by Andrew Murray.

My prayer normally follows the model of the Lord's Prayer; I take each segment and personalize it. A great book on this subject is *Lord, Teach Us to Pray* by Andrew Murray.

I like to follow up my prayer time by listening to the Lord and asking Him to teach me His Word. Sometimes, listening comes during or after my time of Bible reading.

I try to read through the Old Testament once a year and the New Testament two to three times a year. Daily, I read three chapters in the Old Testament, one chapter in Psalms or Proverbs, one chapter in the Gospels, and one chapter in the Epistles. There are days when one chapter will impact me so strongly that I stop there and meditate on it throughout the day.

One more step to help me with Scripture memorization and meditation is to type my notes into my journal at the end of my morning prayers.

A few days a week, I like to worship and intercede for my neighborhood while I run and walk. I head out the door with praise music and run for thirty minutes while praising God. Then as I walk back I intercede for Turkey and the people who live around me. On the days when I don't run, I stop for ten to thirty minutes midday to "keep my heart in tune," as the old song "Whisper a Prayer" suggests. I can feel my need to stop and refocus on God, to abide in Him.

At night I pray for about an hour. I specifically thank the Lord for the answers to prayer for that day. It has been faith-building to recall all He has done each and every day. Our mission mentors taught Stan and me always to read the Bible and a book that inspired us to pray, so at night I read a biography or inspirational book and finish my evening with a Psalm.

Nothing is rigid in my schedule. I move around, I kneel, I walk, I read different versions of the Bible because staying focused is not easy. Intercession is work—but work with great blessing. Although I have a daily structure to my prayers, it is the Lord's time to do with as He wills.

I tell everyone we have
a marriage unlike any other.

WEEK 1
Abide

verb:

TO REMAIN IN PLACE;
TO CONTINUE TO BE SURE
OR FIRM, ENDURE.

DAY 1
ABIDE IN ME

"As the Father has loved me, so have I loved you.
Now remain in my love." John 15:9

*J*esus commands His followers to make disciples of all nations. In other words, He expects us to bear fruit to the ends of the earth. But in His goodness to us, our Lord doesn't merely issue an edict and walk away. He also reveals the secret to fruitfulness: abiding in Him.

In John 15:4–5 (NKJV), Jesus says: "Abide in Me, and I in you. As the branch cannot bear fruit of itself, unless it abides in the vine, neither can you, unless you abide in Me. I am the vine, you are the branches. He who abides in Me, and I in him, bears much fruit; for without Me you can do nothing."

Stan's priority each morning was to spend time with Jesus: worshiping, praying, studying Scripture, journaling, interceding for his neighbors. He viewed these hours as essential to fruitfulness in his mosque community. As he received life from the Vine, he was then able to share life with the lost around him.

Today, meditate on John 15:4–5. Ask the Holy Spirit to show you what it means to abide. In the space below, draw a picture of what abiding looks like, or write your thoughts on abiding. Make a commitment to abide in Jesus.

"Unmapped, unexplored by foreigners, unreached in every way . . . forgotten, until now."

—STAN

EACH AND EVERY DAY

One generation commends your works to another;
they tell of your mighty acts. Psalm 145:4

A biding in Jesus is a daily discipline. The psalmist wrote, "I will praise you every day" (Psalm 145:2, NLT), and Paul encourages believers to pray without ceasing (1 Thessalonians 5:17).

The Stewards dedicated one room of their Istanbul apartment to prayer and study. It featured maps of Turkey, photographs from their many expeditions across the country, and a generous supply of prayer books and devotionals. Stan and Ann purchased several prayer rugs for this room, and one such rug was in relatively poor condition. Stan spent hours repairing its tassels: untying knots, removing twists, straightening threads. Once this remedial work was finished, daily combing kept the tassels straight and free of tangles.

The process reminded Stan of his inner life: "If I didn't spend time keeping my spirit in line with God's plan, a lot of knots and tangles would begin to form. But each and every day, I allow God to comb through the tassels of my soul, and He keeps everything in line."[3]

Today, ask the Father to give you a hunger to abide in Jesus every day. Commit to wake up earlier or to rearrange your schedule—whatever it takes to spend more time with Him. Write a prayer of commitment below.

MORNING DEW

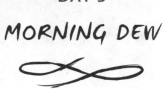

Who is wise? Let them realize these things. Who is discerning? Let them understand. The ways of the LORD are right; the righteous walk in them. . . . Hosea 14:9

I will spend my mornings in prayer," Stan wrote in his prayer journal. "I will close out my day in prayer. When I hear the call to prayer, I will go into my room and pray for Turks."

Jesus began each day in prayer. David started his day by seeking and worshiping his Lord. Men and women of God through the centuries have followed the same pattern. In his prayer journal, Stan compared morning prayer to dew (Hosea 14:5; Psalm 133:3):

"When we lived in San Diego, we set our automatic sprinklers to water the lawn just before dawn. This was the optimal time for the lawn to absorb water. San Diego is a hot climate, and watering in the heat of the day can burn the grass, or the water could dissipate too quickly. But in the stillness of the morning, before the heat of the day, the water could be slowly and fully used by the grass."

Today, as you pray, ask for the refreshing, life-giving dew of the Holy Spirit. And as you continue through this journal, dedicate the first part of your day to abiding in Jesus. Write the steps you might take to ensure that you spend time in God's presence each morning.

"Let fountains of truth erupt out of this floor . . . so that these people will see You and hear You and know You."

—STAN

DAY 4

ABIDING PRACTICES

I rise before dawn and cry for help; I have put
my hope in your word. Psalm 119:147

*I*n *The Live Dead Journal*, missionary and author, Dick Brogden, defines abiding as *"spending extravagant time with Jesus every day."* [4] He encourages his readers to tithe their time to Jesus, to spend two and a half hours each day with Him. Such a deep commitment sounds intimidating—impossible, even—but we could say that variety is the spice of abiding.

As we can see in the introduction to this journal, Stan and Ann incorporated many spiritual disciplines into their abiding times; abiding is much more than presenting an endless list of requests to God. Some common abiding practices include Bible reading, worship, praying for the salvation of your family and friends (or even people you've never met), journaling, praying in the Spirit, meditating on and memorizing Scripture, listening for the voice of the Holy Spirit. Stan even changed his physical posture depending on his activity.

Today, as you pray, listen for the voice of the Spirit. Is Jesus asking for a tithe of your time? Ask the Spirit to show you which of these practices you should include in your abiding time and then record your thoughts below.

"To know the will of God, we need an open Bible and an open map."

—WILLIAM CAREY

AT THE ALTAR

"As for me and my household, we will serve
the LORD." Joshua 24:15

In *Dying Out Loud*, Stan recalled that he was just five years old when
God first spoke to him. It happened at the altar of his grandfather's
church, and the location of this event became extremely significant in
Stan's life.

> The altar would come to represent . . . a place to wait patiently
> for God, a place to seek His will. Throughout my life I've spent
> a lot of time praying at the altar in a variety of churches, and it's
> often been the place where God has spoken to me.[5]

When their children were still babies, Stan and Ann instituted a practice
in their home they called family altar. Each night, they gathered, talked
about the day, sang hymns, and prayed together—thanking God
for prayers answered that day and asking Him for His presence and
provision for the next.

Today, consider whether any physical location in your daily life would be appropriate for a personal "altar"—a place to meet daily with Jesus. As you pray, offer yourself as a living sacrifice to God (Romans 12). Meditate on what it means to be a living sacrifice and record your insights below.

Then, if possible, rearrange your physical surroundings as needed to accommodate an "altar."

"We expect signs and wonders.
We expect to be overcomers.
We expect darkness to flee."

—STAN

DAY 6

MAKE ME USABLE

"Before praying, 'Lord, use me,' pray, 'Lord, make me usable.'" —Calvin Olson

A quick reading of Stan's journal reveals his greatest ambition in life. His prayer, his goal, his desire was to be used by God to reach the unreached—however and wherever his Master saw fit. He wrote:

"Wouldn't it be exciting if our last days were climactic in our relationship with God, rather than a quiet fading away? I want to go down swinging and fighting. I want to go out at the top of my game and not be carried off the field to fade away in spiritual obscurity. I want to go out with dirt in my mouth, with my knuckles bleeding and bruised for the King."

Being used by God is thrilling, but it should also humble us that the Creator of the universe would find us usable and worthy of His attention. Being made usable can be a long and painful process, but it should be the goal of every servant of Jesus. As we abide in Him, He makes us more like Himself. As we abide in Him, He makes us usable.

Today, pray, "Lord, use me to fulfill Your purposes in the world. But first, do whatever it takes to make me usable." Ask the Holy Spirit to show you the areas in your life that must be refined in order for you to be a useful and usable instrument in the hands of Jesus. Record your thoughts below.

PRUNING

Since we are surrounded by such a great cloud of witnesses, let us throw off everything that hinders and the sin that so easily entangles. And let us run with perseverance the race marked out for us. Hebrews 12:1

The fig tree was growing rapidly, out of control, threatening to overwhelm a corner of the yard. Stan realized he had to do something, for the health of the tree and a future harvest of figs. So he cut it back to little more than a stump, hoping he hadn't killed it.

At the altar of his church the next night, Stan prayed a prayer that changed the course of his family's life: "God, I want more. I want You to prune me just like I pruned that fig tree yesterday. Just cut the extra stuff out of my life. Cut it out and let me focus on You and the plans You have for our family."[6]

God answered Stan's prayer. He removed the "extra stuff"—the career, the mortgage, the cultural expectations—so Stan and his family could pursue God's plan without distraction. Hebrews 12:1 encourages believers to "throw off everything that hinders." Sometimes, as God prunes us, He asks us to set aside what we might consider to be good things in order to fulfill His perfect plan.

Today, as you abide in Jesus, ask Him to prune you. Ask Him to begin cutting away the extra, unnecessary parts of your life—for your spiritual health and for the sake of the spiritual fruit you might bear. Below, write about the things—possessions, unhealthy relationships, sin, dreams, ambitions—He is telling you must go.

"The possibility that we are the first believers to walk in these dark places demands our greatest diligence."

—STAN

"God, give me a spirit and will
that are totally abandoned to you."

—STAN

WEEK 2

Surrender

verb:

TO YIELD (SOMETHING)
TO THE POSSESSION
OR POWER OF ANOTHER

DAY 8

I AM YOURS

Were the whole realm of nature mine,
That were a present far too small;
Love so amazing, so divine,
Demands my soul, my life, my all.
—"When I Survey the Wondrous Cross"
by Isaac Watts

The Steward family regularly sang hymns as part of their family altar time, and many of their favorites speak about giving all to Jesus. Stan's journal reveals that *surrender* was a recurring theme of his prayer life:

"Once again, I come to you today, Lord, and say that I am yours. My hopes, dreams, family, reputation, character, wants, desires—all are Yours to do with as You see best. I trust You. Give me peace and trust where I fail to possess them."

Today, as you abide in Jesus, ask Him to show you any areas of your life that you have not been willing to surrender. Are you having trouble trusting Him with your family? With your career? Ask Him for peace and trust in these areas, and write your insights below. As a reminder of your commitment to surrender all to Jesus, write "I Am Yours" on a piece of paper or a notecard and put it in a place where you will see it often.

"Very few people
in the villages of
the Dark Canyon
have ever heard
of the gospel."

—STAN

A RIGID PATH

I consider everything a loss because of the surpassing worth of knowing Christ Jesus my Lord, for whose sake I have lost all things. Philippians 3:8

American consumer culture exerts constant pressure on followers of Jesus. Stan knew from experience that cultural expectations of living a "responsible" life can take us off the path God intended for us.

> We're bombarded with a multitude of messages: "Color inside the lines. Stay inside the box. Think responsibly. What are you going to be when you grow up? How are you going to make a living that will support a family?" Before you know it, you have a career, a mortgage, two car payments . . . and a rigid path set in front of you.[7]

In his journal, Stan said that a God-centered life is often found off of this path: "We are programmed to work hard so we can someday enjoy life and the good things that we have earned. But if you try to find a biblical model for this way of life, you will come up empty. . . . I believe that real living is found in abandonment to God and His purpose and not in our success, income, dreams, plans, hopes, or abilities."

Today, as you pray, ask the Holy Spirit to point out pressures and expectations of your culture that undermine your ability to pursue God's will. What are some things that your culture says are important —such as leisure, retirement, attaining and maintaining a certain lifestyle—but are of little or no value in the kingdom? Surrender these pressures to Jesus and write your insights below. If God is asking you to make changes in your lifestyle, take concrete steps to follow Him in obedience.

"Help me to find
blessing and contentment
in living for You."

—STAN

A SERVANT'S HEART

Serve one another humbly in love.
Galatians 5:13

Servanthood runs counter to our culture and human nature. If we're honest with ourselves, we'll admit that much of the time we would prefer to be served. In the kingdom, however, we are called to serve, to place others ahead of ourselves. We must surrender our desires. Jesus is our example. He said, "For even the Son of Man did not come to be served, but to serve, and to give his life as a ransom for many" (Mark 10:45).

In his prayer journal, Stan wrote, "I want to vigorously cultivate a servant's heart. My daily longing is to have my desires, wants, plans, hopes, and dreams torn out of my heart, and their void to be filled with the desires, wants, plans, hopes, and dreams of God. I want to die to self, to recognition, to status, to selfishness, to glory. I want to serve—not be served. Help me to keep this longing for genuine servanthood fresh and persistent each day."

Today, as you abide in Jesus, surrender your desire to be served and ask Him to give you a longing to lay down your life to serve others. Ask the Holy Spirit to show you practical ways to serve people in your life and record your insights below.

TRUE ABANDONMENT

"The most important thing about any one of us is not what we do but what God does, not what we do for God but what God does for us." —Eugene Peterson

*T*rue abandonment to God does not keep a tally of sacrifice or hardship," Stan wrote in his prayer journal. "True sacrifice does not consider itself a loss; rather, it is characterized by a longing and urgency for more of God. . . . I want the life that says, 'Nothing stands in the way or rivals my focus on fulfilling the purpose for which God has created me.'"

Stan understood that hardship and suffering would eventually equip him to fulfill that purpose. As the apostle Paul wrote: "We can rejoice, too, when we run into problems and trials, for we know that they help us develop endurance. And endurance develops strength of character, and character strengthens our confident hope of salvation" (Romans 5:3–5, NLT).

Today, in your abiding time, pray for the strength
to live a life abandoned to God's purposes. Pray for the
grace to rejoice when trials come. Thank the Lord that
He doesn't waste our hardships but uses them
to develop endurance, character, and hope. Meditate
on these verses in Romans and write about
the truths the Spirit speaks to you.

"I want to die to self,
to recognition, to status,
to selfishness, to glory."

—STAN

LIKE A CANDLE

"My Father, if it is possible, may this cup be taken
from me. Yet not as I will, but as you will."
Matthew 26:39

Paul wrote in 1 Corinthians 15:31 (NKJV), "I die daily." John the
Baptizer said of Jesus, "He must become greater and greater, and
I must become less and less" (John 3:30, NLT). This daily dying to self
means that the will and plan of Jesus continually grow in our hearts and
minds while our dreams and desires dissolve to nothing. As we make a
practice of abiding in Jesus, eventually His desires and passions become
our own.

In his journal, Stan compared this abandoned, crucified life with a
candle. He prayed, "Give me the strength to live as a wick that gives
light only as it dies."

Today, as you pray, light a candle and watch the wick shrink as it burns. Meditate on what it means to die to self. How can dying to self—surrendering our hopes, dreams, and agendas—give light to those around us? Write or draw your thoughts below.

"Praying, true praying, costs an outlay of serious attention and of time, which flesh and blood do not relish."

—E. M. BOUNDS

ALL WILL SUFFER

It has been granted to you on behalf of Christ not only to
believe in him, but also to suffer for him.
Philippians 1:29

The question that God asked Ann is such an important one for this
generation: 'Are you willing to suffer?' The truth is, all of us will
suffer, whether or not we're willing. If we approach suffering with an
unwilling heart, if we fight against it and seek to avoid it at all cost, it can
destroy us. But if we're willing to suffer, if we're open to what God can
accomplish through our suffering, then our joy and hope will be evident
to everyone around us."[8]

Stan understood that even this willingness to suffer comes as a gift from
God. It's not something we attain on our own. In his journal, he wrote, "I
have always thought I could suffer for Christ, as long as I could choose
the 'suffering.' Giving my family to God to 'do as He sees best' for them
is a standard of my daily prayer life. It also, sometimes, scares me."

Today, as you abide in Jesus, examine your heart. Invite the Holy Spirit to show you whether you have been unwilling to suffer for Him. What scares you most about possible suffering? The One who suffered unjustly on our behalf will give us the grace to endure—and the joy to bring glory to Him. What would suffering for Jesus look like in your life? Surrender to Him your ideas of comfort and security, and process your thoughts in the space below.

"God, let me see them the way You see them."

—STAN

DAY 14

COUNT THE COST

"I consider my life worth nothing to me; my only aim is to finish the race and complete the task the Lord Jesus has given me—the task of testifying to the good news of God's grace." Acts 20:24

Anything worth something has a cost," Stan said in *Dying Out Loud*. In the same way that precious things cannot be bought without large sums of money, important transitions cannot happen unless someone pays the price.

> Luke 14:28 says, "Suppose one of you wants to build a tower. Won't you first sit down and estimate the cost to see if you have enough money to complete it?" What would you like to see happen in the lives of those around you? Have you counted the cost? [9]

In his journal, Stan contemplated the cost of being light in a dark place, of treasuring Jesus in the midst of a mosque community: "To pray at the heart of the enemy's camp, to praise the name of Jesus at the altar of Islam, is an honor that few Christians have had—not because it's rare, but because it is often too hard to invest the time and love to find favor in the community.... It is not an area where a few short years will pay off in big dividends. We believe it takes a commitment to dig in one spot long enough to hit bottom."

Today, in the space below, answer Stan's question: What would you like to see God do in the people in your life? List three to five people, and write a prayer for each of them. As you pray, contemplate what it will cost you to see this happen. Will it cost you hours, as you pray more often for them or spend more time with them? Will it cost you your reputation, as you proclaim the Word of God? Will it cost you comfort, as you attempt something new for the kingdom?

"The Holy Spirit only guides us to those places where our loving and good heavenly Father is waiting for us."

—MARK RENFROE

WEEK 3
Listen

verb

MAKE AN EFFORT
TO HEAR SOMETHING;
BE ALERT AND READY
TO HEAR SOMETHING

DAY 15

OPEN HANDS

"Our ultimate joy comes only from following Christ
all the way to heaven." —Dale Ahlquist

When we have committed to a lifestyle of abiding in Jesus and have surrendered our plans, dreams, and agendas to His will, we are finally in a spiritual environment that is conducive to hearing His voice.

In his journal, Stan wrote, "I want to worship God with abandonment . . . to abandon everything that stands in the way of being worshipfully obedient to His plan and purpose for me and my family. . . . God, give me a spirit and will that are totally abandoned to You."

Living with true abandonment is more than a one-time event; it's a daily decision. Some followers of Jesus find it helpful to incorporate specific physical postures in their daily prayers to emphasize surrender and submission, such as kneeling or lying facedown on the floor.

Another practice is to pray with open hands, offering to God both the things He has given us (health, family, vocation) and the things He has not given us (fear, condemnation, doubt). After emptying our hands, we are free to receive what He wants to give us for that day.

Today, in your abiding time, practice the prayer of open hands. Show Jesus that you hold tightly to nothing but Him. Then quietly receive from Him. What is He speaking to you? Where is He leading? Record your thoughts below.

"The opportunity to love on Muslims from the inside of the culture is a unique thing."

—STAN

WE ASKED GOD

"I am the LORD your God, who teaches you what is best
for you, who directs you in the way you should go."
Isaiah 48:17

One of Stan's favorite quotations comes from David Livingstone, the well-known medical missionary to Africa in the nineteenth century. "I am ready to go anywhere," Livingstone said, "provided it be forward."

For Stan, shortly after arriving in Turkey, "forward" meant east—to the border regions near Iran, Iraq, and Syria, areas populated by shepherds, nomads, and warlords. "I thought we should go," Stan said, "so we asked God about it."

After praying about the possibility, the Stewards sensed the Lord was giving them a green light. "We came to a conclusion: We wouldn't know exactly what it would look like, but we knew it was where God was leading us. We made plans to head east." [10]

Today, in your abiding time, think about the decisions you face right now, both large and small. Have you asked God about them? In the space below, list two or three circumstances in which you need direction, and write what the Holy Spirit speaks to you.

"I can't escape the passion and vision we have carried this last year to buy a village house in the Dark Canyon of the Euphrates and open a house of light and prayer."

—STAN

DISCOVER THE TRACK

Whether you turn to the right or to the left,
your ears will hear a voice behind you, saying,
"This is the way; walk in it." Isaiah 30:21

Whenever the Stewards prepared for one of their Silk Road expeditions into central and eastern Turkey, they committed the entire process to prayer. They wanted nothing less than to be led by the Spirit on every trail they followed and in every village they visited. And after receiving direction from God, they moved ahead with purpose.

In a newsletter just before an expedition in 2012, Stan wrote, "We will be attempting to reach the most remote villages in the whole of Anatolia. We are told by the locals that most of these places have never been seen by Westerners. The possibility that we are the first believers to walk in these dark places demands our greatest diligence.... We expect signs and wonders. We expect to be overcomers. We expect darkness to flee."

In this way, the Steward family followed the pattern of the first missionary in this region of the world. F. B. Meyer wrote: "The apostle Paul did not have to cut or carve his way but simply had to discover the track that God had prepared for his steps from of old. And when he found it, it . . . would be the very pathway for which his character and gifts were most adapted."[11]

Today, as you abide in Jesus, write about a time in your life when you knew you were on the track that God had prepared for you. What were the circumstances that led you to that place? How did you make those decisions? Can you see that God was directing you, even when life was difficult?
If you cannot recall such a time, pray that God would help you to hear His plan for your steps going forward.

"I am ready to go anywhere, provided it be forward."

—DAVID LIVINGSTONE

KEYS TO HEARING

"Call to me and I will answer you, and will tell you great
and hidden things that you have not known."
Jeremiah 33:3 (ESV)

As we ask God for guidance and direction, there are a number of
practices that will declutter our lives and block out the "noise" so we
can hear His voice. Three short prayers in Stan's journal give us a good
place to start:

Lord, help me to understand this: "Be silent." First, turn off the TV, close your
laptop, and walk away from your phone. Finding a place of solitude and
stillness away from the urgent yet unimportant demands of daily life will
show God that time with Him is your priority.

Help me to find full blessing and contentment in living for You. Next, watch your
motives. God is not a vending machine that exists to give us what we want
when we slide our coins into the slot. We must not view our abiding time as
a transaction—even in those moments when we are seeking a specific word
of direction. He is the reward.

Give me a heart that is open to Your lessons and discipline. Finally, adopt an
attitude of humility. A teachable attitude will allow you to hear what God
is saying through the Holy Spirit, Scripture, and other people. Consider
what He might be teaching you in every circumstance you face.

Today, as you pray, examine your motives for abiding in Christ. Are you pursuing Jesus, or are you seeking what He can give you? In the space below, write about Scriptures you have read recently or conversations you have had that God is using to speak to you.

MANY ADVISERS

There is safety in having many advisers.
Proverbs 11:14 (NLT)

A few months after he was diagnosed with terminal cancer, Stan addressed a roomful of friends and colleagues in Istanbul—fellow missionaries serving in Turkey. The talk was typical Stan: passionate, funny, direct. He reflected on his illness, told some stories from his journey, and shared advice on several topics, including mentors.

Stan talked about some of his mentors through the years, such as those mentioned in *Dying Out Loud*: Calvin and Marian Olson, Abdullah, Marc. And he encouraged everyone in the room, no matter how experienced, to find at least one mentor. He even said that one of his mentors—a highly educated and widely published man in his late seventies who has worked in the Muslim world for decades—has a mentor of his own.

Stan's advice is biblical, of course, and is relevant to all of God's people, not just missionaries.

Today, as you abide in Jesus, ask Him to give you mentors, people who will challenge you to grow and will walk alongside you on your journey toward becoming like Christ. Rather than strategizing and thinking analytically, pray, "I trust You, Lord, to lead me to the right mentors." He knows what you need more than you do. As you sense the Holy Spirit giving you names, write them in the space below. Pray for wisdom about how to proceed.

"Those who sow
in tears shall reap
with shouts of joy."

—PSALM 126:5 (ESV)

LEARNING TO WAIT

> "We can count on God to lead us into whatever
> we are to do." —Dallas Willard

The men in Stan and Ann's neighborhood prayed at the local mosque every Friday at midday. As Stan built friendships with these men, some of them invited him to their weekly prayers. Not yet an expert in the culture or Islamic tradition, he was confronted by his own questions: *Could I go to the mosque and pray to Jesus? What kind of message would this send to our community? Would I be welcome there, or would my presence cause unnecessary offense?*

Stan prayed about his options—and he also called four of his mentors to ask them about his situation. Two said, "Absolutely, go for it." The other two said, "Absolutely not. Don't do it."

Because their decision was split, Stan prayed and waited. "I'm not going to force this to happen," he prayed. "I want it to be anointed. I don't want to make a mistake with this." The Lord eventually gave His answer, and Stan walked ahead in faith.[12]

We don't like to wait. Our culture preaches instant gratification, and our consumer infrastructure delivers: fast food, movies on demand, vacation by credit card. This cultural impatience infects our spiritual life, especially when we want guidance or an answer to prayer. But patience is a fruit of the Spirit, a gift available for the asking. In God's *good* time, He will answer.

Today, as you abide in Jesus, ask Him to teach you patience. Ask Him for the wisdom to recognize His timing is best. Ask Him for the endurance to wait for the answer. In the space below, write about a time when it seemed God was slow in responding to your request. Can you now see that His timing was perfect?

"The harvest is
plentiful but the
workers are few.
Ask the Lord of the
harvest, therefore, to
send out workers into
his harvest fields."

—MATTHEW 9:37–38

DAY 21

WHAT HE WANTS

"I have been crucified with Christ and I no longer live, but Christ lives in me." Galatians 2:20

W hen I was growing up," Stan said in *Dying Out Loud*, "the Apollo program was in full swing, and teachers everywhere told children they could be anything they wanted to be. But God impressed on my life that I couldn't become anything I wanted to be—I could become what He wanted me to be."[13]

We have reached the end of Week 3 in our journal, a week dedicated to thoughts about guidance, direction, and hearing the voice of God. This is a scary topic for some. The reality is that many people are content not to hear. They suffer from a "Jonah complex": They are afraid that God will tell them to do something uncomfortable or sacrificial or dangerous.

If this is your fear, it will be helpful to keep in mind one simple fact: Our heavenly Father is good. As Mark Renfroe writes in *Live Dead the Journey*, "Luke 11 directly links the goodness of the Father to the work of the Holy Spirit. The Holy Spirit only guides us to those places where our loving and good heavenly Father is waiting for us."[14]

Today, during your abiding time, use the space below to process your thoughts about who God wants you to be or what He wants you to do. Are you afraid that God will call you to do something you don't want to do? Has this fear kept you from seeking intimacy with Him? Ask Him to remove this fear and to remind you of His goodness.

"You don't measure yourself
by your success, but you
measure yourself against
the unfinished task."

—LOREN TRIPLETT

"God isn't looking for people of great faith, but for individuals ready to follow Him."

—HUDSON TAYLOR

WEEK 4

Follow

verb

STRIVE AFTER; AIM AT

THERE IS MORE

His master replied, "Well done, good and faithful servant!"
Matthew 25:21

There is more. This idea was a recurring theme in Stan's life. He wrote the following paragraphs, found in his prayer journal, at least a decade before his death:

"The heroes of the Bible allowed God to take them out of the status quo. They lived lives that we consider legendary because of their sacrifice, determination, and intensity. But they did something even more amazing—they went further with God.

"A prophet who lost all because of his obedience, a king who repeatedly humbled himself before God, a young Jewish girl who stepped into history by her willingness to lay it all on the line to save her people— these men and women said, 'I want something more.' They did not seek houses, transportation, promotions, plaudits, and power. These legends wanted to be completely used up for the purpose and opportunity of being a tool for God.

"Something inside of them dug deep into the will of God and said, 'This is what I live for.' I can't recall a single one of these who retired and lived a peaceful, enjoyable life. These revolutionaries worked until they dropped, died of illness, or were killed. There are no stories of a grand retirement, because the focus was on God's purpose, not their reward. They didn't have a quiet ending. The trials, troubles, and testing increased as they closed out their days on earth. They grew in power spiritually, they grew in influence and controversy, they grew in effectiveness, until they left this earth in death.

"This is what I want. My heart cries out and longs to be focused only on what God has for me. I want to finish well."

Today, as you abide in Jesus, meditate on the idea of "something more." Can you say of God's will, "This is what I live for?" Where is He leading you, both physically and spiritually? Write a prayer that commits you to going deeper with Him.

DEEPER INTO THE WORLD

> "The spiritual life does not remove us from the world but leads us deeper into it." —Henri Nouwen

The month before Stan was diagnosed with terminal cancer, he was in remote eastern Turkey, with Ann and Stanley, on one of the family's frequent Silk Road expeditions. As he was able, Stan posted updates to his Facebook account. He wrote this dispatch on August 19, 2012:

> "Back to our Euphrates base tonight after a wonderful day of steep roads, dust, steppe, and shepherds. We made it to the end of the road . . . only to find more goat trails to follow. Unmapped, unexplored by foreigners, unreached in every way . . . forgotten, until now. We explored the goat trails until we began to lose the sun. Six new families to add to our circuit, four of them nomadic shepherd clans. Promised to return. . . . Drank lots of warm goat milk mixed with baking soda to seal our new friendship. Overwhelmed at the possibilities."

A lifestyle of abiding gives both the motivation and the ability to move deeper into the world. Stan understood this. As we abide in Jesus, we come to love Him more. As we love Him more, He gives us the passion to share Him with others. And as we step out—sometimes on forgotten goat trails along the ancient Silk Road, sometimes on our school campuses in the suburbs—the Spirit works through us to draw people to Jesus.

Today, in your abiding time, pray for guidance and courage to move deeper into the world. Where, specifically, is God asking you to begin? Ask Him for more of the Holy Spirit, for both the passion and ability to make disciples. Write what you hear the Spirit say to you.

"Real living is
found in abandonment
to God and His purpose
and not in our success,
income, dreams, plans,
hopes, or abilities."

—STAN

WILLING TO LOVE THEM

> "To bless, to save, to help another, will fill our hearts with the most unalloyed blessedness of which the heart is capable." —F. B. Meyer

You don't have to be a saint to live your life out in front of Muslim people," Stan said in *Dying Out Loud.* "You just have to pray every day, *God, let me see them the way You see them.* You just have to be willing to love them."[15]

So how does this work in real life? An excerpt from Stan's journal reveals how love can change perceptions:

"We were first viewed as a novelty: 'This is my American friend.' Then, once we had demonstrated longevity and staying power in the community, we were targets for conversion to Islam. Eventually, we were viewed as good people by some, a mystery to others, and a problem to a few. The weight of the imam's affection for us, along with the mosque elders, has bought us favor from those on the sidelines.

"Currently, there are only a few people we feel would rather not have us around—and even on them God has been working. The most fanatical of those few had a son serving in a hot zone for terrorism. We've traveled in that area and are well known there. During the course of his son's assignment, I would check in several times a week as to his safety.

I called from the States to inquire when I heard of the deaths of soldiers. I counted the days until his discharge, and on August 10, he came home safe. The next time I was at prayer, the father came and knelt next to me to pray. He put his arm around me and hugged me. Perseverance, perseverance, perseverance."

Today, as you pray, consider where God is leading you into deeper community with the lost around you. Is He giving you specific names? What might your involvement look like? What will it cost? Write your thoughts below.

"Never pity missionaries; envy them. They are where the real action is— where life and death, sin and grace, heaven and hell converge."

—ROBERT C. SHANNON

THE DARK CANYON

> "The thief comes only to steal and kill and destroy;
> I have come that they may have life, and have
> it to the full." John 10:10

In Stan's final months, his thoughts were never far from the unreached peoples of Turkey—the ethnolinguistic groups that have little or no access to the gospel, the people groups that will never hear the good news unless we go to them. Here is one of Stan's Facebook posts from October 2012:

> In bed, in the dark for the past three hours, thinking over the last six weeks: From the best Silk Road expedition ever to eight months to live, give or take. Terminal cancer. And yet, I can't escape the passion and vision we have carried this last year to buy a village house in the Dark Canyon of the Euphrates and open a house of light and prayer, a place of pilgrimage for teams who want to intercede for the unreached. . . . Crazy dreams of an (apparently) dying man. Maybe not. . . . I believe with all my heart we can still do this . . . even more so now than before.

In *Dying Out Loud*, Stan said of this area: "This Dark Canyon used to be an ancient shortcut, a part of Turkey where the original Silk Road passed by. The road has been there for a thousand years and passes through village after village after village. . . . Very few of the people in those villages have ever heard of the gospel. They all need someone to come alongside them, to share the good news with them. But it's not going to be reached in a week or two, or even a year or two."[16]

Today, as you abide in Jesus, intercede for the villages of the Dark Canyon of the Euphrates. Pray that followers of Jesus will go there to proclaim the good news, that the gospel will take root in the hard terrain, that churches will spring up and reach the entire region. In the space below, write a prayer for the people of the Dark Canyon.

"We believe it takes
a commitment to dig in
one spot long enough to
hit bottom."

—STAN

STAN'S PRAYER

"Prayer doesn't just change circumstances; more important, it changes us." —Mark Batterson

*L*ooking out over a dark and sleeping city of 17 million, I realize again how blessed I am to live among so many who are lost," Stan posted on Facebook in November 2012. "When I add the villages of the Euphrates to the equation, it makes me weep with hope. . . . My soul sings this morning in Istanbul. I love my purpose."

God called the Steward family to treasure Him among the Muslims of Istanbul. As they loved Him, they grew to love the city of their calling. But how can anyone reach a city with millions of people? Stan, Ann, Elle, and Stanley began by loving and praying for their neighbors: the shopkeeper who sold them their phones, the vegetable sellers in the *pazar*, the guys Stan prayed next to in the neighborhood mosque.[17]

This is how Stan and Stanley prayed for their mosque friends:

> "Dear God, break down the walls of their hearts right now: the man in front of me, the men to each side, the man behind me. Open their eyes, God. Break down the wall of Islam. Demolish this stronghold. Let fountains of truth erupt out of this floor we're kneeling on. Let fountains of truth flow so that these people will see You and hear You and know You. Immediately, right now, imprint on their hearts and minds the name of Jesus.

While they're praying, visit them supernaturally. Stamp the name of Jesus the Savior on their souls. We claim this territory by Your blood, and we drive back the forces of Satan. We drive back the darkness. We destroy the strongholds of Satan in the name of Jesus Christ"[18]

Today, as you abide in Jesus, echo Stan's prayer for his mosque community. Pray for the men who will visit that mosque this week. You don't know their names, but the Father does. In the space below, rewrite this prayer on behalf of every mosque across Turkey.

DAY 27

SOW WITH TEARS

Those who sow in tears shall reap with shouts of joy.
He who goes out weeping, bearing the seed for sowing,
shall come home with shouts of joy, bringing his sheaves
with him. Psalm 126:5–6 (ESV)

Spiritual harvest requires both seed and tears. When the Stewards were sent out as missionaries, the speaker at their commissioning service addressed this reality of the harvest: "[He] said that if we wanted to reap a harvest," Stan said, "we would have to moisten the dry ground with tears over the lost."

When Stan, Ann, Elle, and Stanley arrived in Turkey, they found soil that had been dried out for centuries. Carrying with them the seed of the gospel, they set about moistening the hard, dry ground. As their circle of friends and acquaintances grew, both in Istanbul and in the Euphrates region, they literally wept for the lost. Daily, they shed tears for their neighbors, looking ahead to a joyful harvest.

Stan's ministry of tears continued to his final days. Just weeks before he died, he wrote on Facebook about a friend he loved dearly: "The General showed up to visit me and harry the [hospital] staff to make sure all was being done to meet my needs.... Please pray for the General to meet Jesus and live his remaining days for Christ. He sat on my bed holding my hand and repeatedly kissed it. Oh, God, do not let him be lost!"

Today, as you abide in Jesus, meditate on Psalm 126:5–6. Ask God to break your heart for the lost, to give you His heart for those far from Him. Begin praying for the people in your life who are lost without Jesus and write a prayer for them below.

"My heart cries out and longs to be focused only on what God has for me. I want to finish well."

– STAN

ARE YOU CALLED?

He said to them, "Go into all the world and preach
the gospel to all creation." Mark 16:15

Abdullah's finger jabbed at Stan's chest, while the words jabbed at Stan's heart: "Are you called? . . . Who are you called to?" [19]

God is calling you to someone. He is calling you to pray, to give, to go.

In February 2013, on his Facebook page, Stan quoted author Andrew Murray: "But how much greater the glory of intercession—when a man makes bold to say to God what he desires for others and seeks to bring down on one soul, or it may be on hundreds and thousands, the power of the eternal with all its blessings."

Will you follow Jesus deeper into prayer? Will you seek to bring down the power of the eternal?

In his prayer journal, Stan wrote: "God, challenge us to give freely, sacrificially, without any piousness of spirit. Thank You for giving us a heart to give back to You. You have blessed us so much! You have proved Yourself over and over throughout the years. 'Where your treasure is, there your heart will be also.'" Will you follow Jesus deeper into sacrificial giving? Will you invest your treasure in the mission of making Jesus famous among those who have never heard of Him?

Will you go? "These relationships are the only link to a physical representative of Christ that most of these families have ever had," Stan wrote in his journal. "There is intense oppression from Satan; we are drained physically, spiritually, and mentally after Friday prayers. But the opportunity to love on Muslims from the inside of the culture is a unique thing."

Will you follow Jesus to the ends of the earth? Will you give up your comfort and security to love Muslims in their communities?

Today, as you abide in Jesus, answer these questions:
Am I called? To whom am I called? Am I willing to intercede
for the lost and for those trying to reach them? Am I willing
to give sacrificially so the unreached can hear the gospel?
Am I willing to follow Jesus wherever He leads?

"I have but one candle of life to burn, and I would rather burn it out in a land filled with darkness than in a land flooded with light."

—ION KEITH-FALCONER

NOTES

1. Shawn Smucker, *Dying Out Loud: The Story of a Silk Road Nomad* (Springfield, MO: Influence Resources, 2013), 235.

2. Dick Brogden, *Live Dead Joy: 365 Days of Living and Dying with Jesus* (Springfield, MO: Influence Resources, 2014).

3. Smucker, *Dying Out Loud*, 224.

4. Dick Brogden, ed., *The Live Dead Journal: 30 Days of Prayer for Unreached Peoples* (Springfield, MO: Influence Resources, 2012), 11.

5. Smucker, *Dying Out Loud*, 17.

6. Ibid., 43.

7. Ibid., 19.

8. Ibid., 189.

9. Ibid., 198.

10. Ibid., 95.

11. Ibid., 93.

12. Ibid., 136.

13. Ibid., 21.

14. Dick Brogden, Mike Murray, Charity Reeb, Mark Renfroe, eds. *Live Dead the Journey: An Interactive Prayer Adventure for Unreached People Groups* (Springfield, MO: Influence Resources, 2013), 79.

15. Smucker, *Dying Out Loud*, 237.

16. Ibid., 130.

17. Stan's decision to pray weekly to Jesus in mosques is not standard missiological practice among Christian missionaries, nor does it represent the standard practice of the denomination to which the Stewards belong.

18. Smucker, *Dying Out Loud*, 144–145.

19. Ibid., 39–40

ABOUT THE AUTHOR

Mike Murray was an award-winning journalist before moving to Central Eurasia to work in university ministry and church planting. He and his wife, Nikki, and their three children live in Istanbul, Turkey.

Visit www.DyingOutLoudChallenge.org for more information about

- joining the Dying Out Loud community
- taking a prayer trip to Turkey
- serving as a missionary in Turkey or elsewhere in Eurasia

GET THE BOOK AND DVD

For more information about these resources
please visit www.influenceresources.com